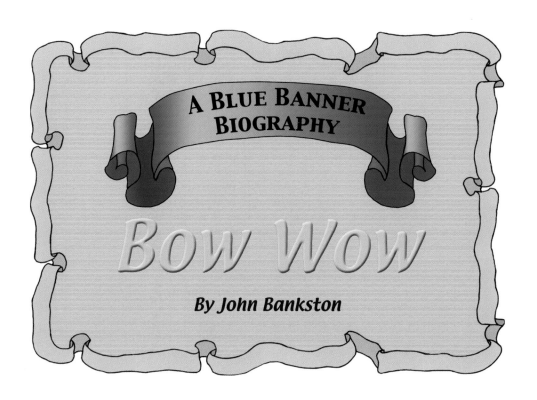

A BLUE BANNER BIOGRAPHY

Bow Wow

By John Bankston

Mitchell Lane
PUBLISHERS

P.O. Box 196
Hockessin, Delaware 19707
Visit us on the web: www.mitchelllane.com
Comments? email us: mitchelllane@mitchelllane.com

Printing   2   3   4   5   6   7   8   9

Blue Banner Biographies

Library of Congress Cataloging-in-Publication Data
Bankston, John, 1974-
        Bow Wow / John Bankston.
            p. cm. — (A blue banner biography)
Includes bibliographical references (p.   ) and index.
Discography: p.
Filmography: p.
Contents: The break — Death Row deals — The "Lil" career — The sophomore slump? — Not Lil
    Anymore.
        ISBN 1-58415-220-6 (library bound)
    1. Bow Wow (Musician)—Juvenile literature. 2. Rap musicians—United States—Biography—
Juvenile literature. [1. Bow Wow (Musician) 2. Rap musicians. 3. African Americans—Biogra-
phy.] I. Title. II. Series.
        ML3930.B64 B3 2003
        782.421649'092--dc22

                                                                                            2003024036

ABOUT THE AUTHOR: Born in Boston, Massachussetts, **John Bankston** began publishing articles in newspapers and magazines while still a teenager. Since then, he has written over two hundred articles, and contributed chapters to books such as *Crimes of Passion,* and *Death Row 2000,* which have been sold in bookstores across the world. He has written numerous biographies for young adults, including *Eminem* and *Nelly* (Mitchell Lane). He currently lives in Portland, Oregon.
PHOTO CREDITS: Cover: Scott Gries/Getty Images; p. 4 Jamie Squire/Getty Images; p. 6 Getty Images; p. 12 Kevin Winter/Getty Images; p. 15 Paul Skipper/Globe Photos, Inc.; p. 17 Clinton H. Wallace/Globe Photos, Inc.; p. 20 Reuters NewMedia Inc./Corbis; p. 24 Milan Ryba/Globe Photos, Inc.; p. 26 Scott Gries/Getty Images; p. 28 AP Photo/Terry Gilliam
ACKNOWLEDGMENTS: The following story has been thoroughly researched, and to the best of our knowledge, represents a true story. While every possible effort has been made to ensure accuracy, the publisher will not assume liability for damages caused by inaccuracies in the data, and makes no warranty on the accuracy of the information contained herein. This story has not been authorized nor endorsed by Shad Moss (Bow Wow).

CONTENTS

Shad Moss has been performing in front of crowds since he was very young. He started out in front of his family and in talent shows, and when he was six, he rapped for an entire audience at a Snoop Dogg tour.

The Break

*T*he crowd began to cheer. Shad felt himself being lifted up—over his mother's head, over the heads of the fans. Suddenly he was on stage. Looking out into the audience, he saw the thousands of people there for his heroes—for Snoop Dogg and Dr. Dre. Now they were all waiting—waiting for him.

During a break between sets for musicians, fans were asked if they wanted to get up on stage and rap. Most of them weren't very good. So when Shad approached the microphone, nobody was expecting much.

They were about to be surprised.

He wasn't very nervous. He'd done this before, at local talent shows and in his living room. Now it was Shad's time to shine.

"He'd pick up my kitchen utensils and combs and brushes and start rapping," his mother, Theresa

Snoop Dogg (right) heard Shad perform when Shad was just six years old. He called Shad Lil Bow Wow and invited Shad to tour with him.

Caldwell, told *Jet Magazine.* "I noticed it was something he liked and he just progressed as he got older."

By that evening in 1993, Shad was ready. He freestyled, making up the rhymes as he went along. Soon the audience began to clap, keeping the beat set by the kid with the microphone.

After his set, Shad was rushed backstage. The head-liner wanted to meet him.

Snoop Dogg's tour was named after his latest album. He was the reason Shad's mother bought tickets, and part of the reason Shad started rapping.

Snoop had heard Shad's performance. He was impressed. Until then Shad's stage name had been Kid Gangsta. Backstage the older hip-hop star looked at Shad and saw something familiar. He saw the same energy, the same stage confidence, and the same skills he had.

He looked at Shad and gave him a new name: Lil Bow Wow. Snoop had just one question for the new kid: Would he like to join the tour?

Shad was on his way. He was six years old.

Shad Gregory Moss was born on March 9, 1987, in Columbus, Ohio, but his father Alfonso Moss left soon after. Shad was an only child.

Raising her son without any help wasn't easy. For a while, Theresa worked three jobs—at a reception desk, at a department store, and in a gas station. Shad didn't see his mother much.

Rapper Snoop Dogg looked at Shad and gave him a new name: Lil Bow Wow.

"I refused to let my son grow up the way I grew up," Theresa explained to *Ebony*. "Bow had to grow up fast. I was young, I couldn't afford a babysitter. Bow had to stay home by himself at three years old. I had to do what I had to do."

Alone, Shad used his imagination. Most kids his age pretended to be sports stars, police officers, or firefighters. Shad pretended to be a rapper.

Hip-hop music was the sound track for Shad's life. He listened to everyone from Snoop Dogg to Jay-Z, his tastes influenced by his mother. He heard it in the car and in the living room. He watched rappers on TV and listened to them on the CDs Theresa played.

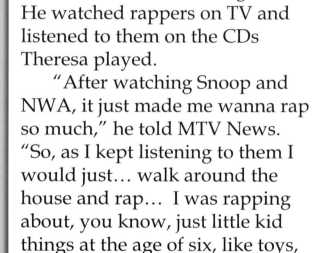

Shad made up the stage name Kid Gangsta, and got his mother to sign him up for local talent contests.

"After watching Snoop and NWA, it just made me wanna rap so much," he told MTV News. "So, as I kept listening to them I would just… walk around the house and rap… I was rapping about, you know, just little kid things at the age of six, like toys, school, '1, 2, 3,' stuff like that."

He made up the stage name Kid Gangsta, and got Theresa to sign him up for local talent contests. He won a few, but Shad was just getting started.

Snoop Dogg was coming to Columbus. Shad begged his mom to take him to the concert. Along with former NWA member Dr. Dre, Snoop was promoting The Chronic Tour. Named after Snoop's album, a celebration of a potent form of the illegal drug marijuana, The Chronic Tour wasn't a place most parents would consider taking their six-year-old.

Then again, Theresa wasn't most parents. She took Shad everywhere. Besides, babysitters were expensive.

During a pause in the show, the announcer's voice carried over the crowd. Did anyone want to come up and rap?

Shad's hand shot up. That moment, his life changed.

After a few hours backstage, hanging out with Snoop and meeting other performers, Shad was asked to join them. Theresa agreed.

For the rest of the summer, Shad (now known as Lil Bow Wow) played before packed stadiums. When the summer ended, so did the tour. It was time to go back to school and play with kids his age. Except Shad still wanted to rap. He wanted to follow in the footsteps of his hero, Snoop Dogg. Soon he'd follow him all the way to Death Row.

At age six, Shad was rapping in front of packed stadiums as part of Snoop Dogg's Chronic Tour.

Death Row Deals

*B*ack home in Columbus, Shad tried to enjoy the kinds of things most six-year-olds enjoy. He played video games and rode his bike. He made new friends at school. As his manager, Theresa received a percentage of Shad's income; the rest was in the bank waiting for him to turn 18.

While money was less of a problem than it had been, Shad missed the life he'd had that summer. It's tough to be a normal six-year-old when you've spent your summer vacation entertaining thousands of people.

Finally, Shad got the call he'd been waiting for. Snoop Dogg wanted him to record a song for his next album, *Doggystyle.* With luck, maybe he could sign a contract with the label Snoop performed for, Death Row Records.

Not many people would imagine a preteen rapper like Lil Bow Wow joining Death Row Records. The label's artists mainly produced CDs with Parental Advisory labels on the front. Along with Snoop, Death Row's other hip-hop stars were known for a type of rap often referred to as "gangsta rap." This hip-hop style was named for its aggressive beats and lyrics about violence and gang life. One of its best-known stars, Tupac Shakur, was shot to death on a Las Vegas street in 1996.

Rapping on Snoop's album required Shad to memorize someone else's words, and then say them perfectly.

Label founder Marion "Suge" Knight didn't want Shad to be a "Kid Gangsta." He knew most parents were reluctant to buy the music his artists released. Many of their CDs went unheard by younger hip-hop fans.

A huge audience wasn't listening to Death Row. Knight thought Shad could change that. Pop music's boy bands and teen singers like *NSync and Britney Spears were becoming famous and making millions of dollars. Knight was sure Lil Bow Wow could do the same thing.

For Shad, rapping on Snoop's album was a world apart from freestyling on stage. He had to memorize someone else's words, and then say them again and again, perfectly. This wasn't easy.

Shad is shown here performing at the Source Hip Hop Music Awards. He was 13 years old and had just released his debut album Beware of Dog.

"I was in the studio with Snoop, and he had written something for me," Shad explained to Billboard.com. "I really couldn't get it. They were yelling at me and I didn't like it. I wanted to quit. I went back home and studied that rap. I went back the next day and showed them I could do it."

Los Angeles gave Shad more than just recording experience. Another Ohio native gave Lil Bow Wow his next big break. At the time, Arsenio Hall hosted one of the most popular talk shows on late-night television.

Future president Bill Clinton even played the saxophone during a guest appearance. By the early 1990s, almost every actor or actress with a movie coming out was appearing on the show.

When Shad performed, he was seen by millions. People were beginning to recognize his name. Although he was in elementary school, he started getting into nightclubs and going to parties. He often bumped into Jermaine Dupri.

Based out of Atlanta, Dupri had been a producer for the kid duo Kris Kross. Better known for their backwards pants than their rapping, the pair had a major hit with the song "Jump."

Shad knew Dupri could help him with his debut. The producer wasn't interested. He wanted a performer with a career, not another one-hit-wonder novelty act.

Shad knew Jermaine Dupri could help him with his debut. But the producer wasn't interested.

Soon, Dupri's lack of interest wouldn't matter. Death Row's Knight seemed to live the life his artists rapped about. He was sentenced to nine years in jail for assault. Without Knight, most of the artists left the label. It quickly ran out of money.

Shad's dreams of a music career seemed to go out the door as well. Without a label or a deal, he returned to Columbus, Ohio.

The "Lil" Career

*A*fter freestylin' on stage and sharing a recording studio with Snoop Dogg, adjusting to school and life back in Columbus, Ohio, was even harder than before. All Shad Moss wanted to do was make music. Unfortunately, Death Row founder Marion Knight had legal problems. He didn't have time for a nine-year-old with ambition. And despite earlier talk of expanding his label's audience, Knight never offered Shad a contract.

Shad wanted one.

"Bow was devastated," Shad's mother told *The New York Times Magazine.* "He'd say, 'Please call Snoop, Mommy. Tell him I want to come back out there.' But when I'd call up Death Row Records, they were like, 'We don't know no Bow Wow.' Click."

The harsh sound of a dial tone seemed like the last note for Shad's career. Snoop came to the rescue. After

Knight was handed a prison sentence, Snoop left the label. Soon after, he gave Theresa the number of another record executive.

Steve Prudholme worked at Epic Records, a division of Sony. After listening to Lil Bow Wow's music and watching a tape of the young rapper's performance, he sent the material to a music producer in Atlanta: Jermaine Dupri.

When he'd met Shad in Los Angeles, Dupri didn't think he wanted to produce him. After watching the

Shad's mother Theresa (right) is also his manager. Before Shad's career could support them, Theresa had to work three jobs.

tape, he changed his mind. Any doubt he had was erased when he put Shad up during a Jay-Z show. Both the hip-hop star and the producer agreed that Shad had the skills and stage presence of an adult. By then Dupri realized Shad could do something more than just make music.

"These days in rap, little kids don't have any role models," Dupri explained to *Jet* magazine. "I knew it was time for him to come out because little girls from eleven to sixteen didn't have anybody who they could claim as their own."

In 1998, Shad and his mother relocated to a home near Dupri's Atlanta recording studio. As Shad's professional life took off, his personal life changed too. His mother met and married Rodney Caldwell. Suddenly he had a stepfather and two stepsisters, Tishana and Saquanna.

Shad didn't have much time to be upset about no longer being an only child. He was too busy working. Dupri had been guiding young hip-hop stars from the time he was nineteen. Besides Kris Kross, he'd produced talents from Usher Raymond to Destiny's Child. He wanted Shad to have a lasting career. He realized Shad's vocal skills were stronger than Kris Kross's had been — in interviews

> *Jermaine Dupri realized Shad could do something more than just make music.*

Jermaine Dupri (left) originally did not want to be Shad's producer. He changed his mind, however, when he saw Shad perform in front of a crowd.

Dupri claimed they had never rapped on stage until he worked with them.

Dupri convinced Theresa to let Dupri's father, Michael Mauldin, and his sister, Lucy Raoof, comanage her son's career. She was nervous about giving up control, but quickly realized that without Dupri's help, Shad might not have a career at all. She agreed, so long as she could remain involved. Besides, Dupri seemed to be like the older brother Shad never had. She needed to trust him.

In 2000, Lil Bow Wow's debut CD, *Beware of Dog,* was released. With Dupri's production, guest vocals from well-known artists like Snoop, and Shad's own trademark voice and fast raps, the CD was an immediate hit.

Shad's double-time delivery reminded many listeners of Ohio rap group Bone Thugs-n-Harmony. That wasn't the only reason for its success.

"When it comes to little guys or guys period, if the girls think they are cute, that's the first key. This business is show business," Dupri told *Jet.* "It's all about people looking at you. If you have something that is automatic that makes people look at you, you've got one half of your foot through the door."

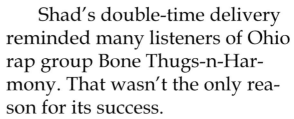

When the single "Bounce With Me" hit number one, Shad became the youngest person in history to have a top single.

Shad's first CD didn't just get his foot in the door. It sold over two million copies. When the single "Bounce With Me" hit number one, Shad became the youngest person in history to have a top single. He even earned a listing in *The Guinness Book of World Records.*

Yet while his album went double platinum, many asked the same question. Was he another Kris Kross? Would he have a musical career or be a one-hit wonder? The answer would be in his next CD.

The Sophomore Slump?

Shad "Lil Bow Wow" Moss was under five feet tall. He wore a diamond-encrusted Mickey Mouse pendant. Everything about him seemed designed to appeal to kids. Even at 13, Shad realized how important it was to be a role model.

"I do have a responsibility, and that is to always stay positive like I am," he told MTV.com. "I don't curse, so fans can just listen to the album. That's my main thing . . . to stay focused and positive."

His effect on fans could be overwhelming. After all, he was still a student at Reynoldsburg Junior High, trying to get good grades and even earning school awards for writing. Barely a teenager, he also got to take part in entertainment industry awards. At the MTV Movie Awards he and *Dawson's Creek* actress Katie Holmes were co-presenters. At the Grammys he "drove" the limousine Madonna left in.

And he felt the love and the craziness whenever he did a mall promotion.

At Chicago's Evergreen Plaza, the crush of mainly female fans filled every inch of available space. He watched in astonishment as they screamed his name, snapped pictures, and begged for autographs. It got so out of control that eventually the mall had to close.

Afterward he told *Jet*, "I really thought it was crazy. To be in a position where if I do one little thing, every-

Shad is shown here performing at the BET Awards in 2001. His song "What's My Name" won him a Viewer's Choice Award.

thing just shuts down, it's something. I was really happy about that and happy no one got hurt."

At his age, it was easy to believe in forever. But Shad's producer, Jermaine Dupri, knew that as quickly as fans embraced a music star, they moved on to the next big thing. Follow-up CDs often were sold from discount bins. Kris Kross's debut, *Totally Krossed Out*, sold four million copies. Their next release flopped. So as Dupri and Shad worked on his second album, the shadow of the sophomore slump was a threatening storm cloud hanging over every decision.

Shad had spent the summer headlining the Scream Tour, a long way from freestyling during the Chronic Tour seven years earlier. "The only bad thing about it is that you miss out . . . ," Shad confessed to the Yahoo music site Launch.com, "like when I go home, I talk to my friends and I haven't seen any of my boys for I don't know how many years, ever since elementary school, so it's kinda hard."

> *Instead of returning to school, Shad now had a full-time tutor. Atlanta became as much of a home to him as Columbus.*

Returning to Dupri's Atlanta studio, Shad didn't have much time to visit with friends. A full-time tutor replaced going to school. Atlanta became as much of a home to Shad as Columbus.

Dupri brought in new producers, the Neptunes, who'd worked with many pop stars. They helped increase the album's mass appeal. The extra effort paid off. Released in 2001, *Doggy Bag* went platinum, selling over a million copies its first month. It's first single, the ballad "Thank You," was written because, as Shad told *Jet Magazine,* "I felt like I wanted to tell everyone how much I appreciated the love they gave me on the first album. I was real happy and I wanted everyone to know."

Shad and Jermaine stayed happy. Lil Bow Wow's second release sold nearly as well as the first — a huge accomplishment when many sophomore CDs do poorly. But Shad wasn't going to be content just making music.

On his second album, Shad worked with the Neptunes to increase the album's mass appeal.

Not Lil Anymore

*S*had "Lil Bow Wow" Moss's first two albums sold four million copies. He'd headlined a pair of concert tours, Scream and Scream 2, performing before thousands of fans.

There seemed to be just one thing left to do: act.

Rappers becoming actors is nothing new. Former NWA member Ice Cube, along with Ice-T and LL Cool J, have all had successful acting careers. They've attracted movie audiences who might not listen to their music. Shad was younger than they were, but that was an advantage. After all, teenagers buy millions of movie tickets.

"If you're a hot artist things like this are going to come automatically," he explained to *The New York Times.* "It's kind of easy nowadays."

Like rapper Will Smith, Shad started small—on the small screen of television and in smaller parts in movies. He played Jalil in *Carmen: A Hip-Hopera* opposite Beyoncé Knowles of Destiny's Child on MTV. He had a role in *All About the Benjamins.* His chance to be a star arrived with a movie about hoop dreams written just for him.

"The inspiration was Bow Wow," Michael Elliot admitted in an interview with *Variety.* Elliot had just

Shad participated in a basketball training camp in Los Angeles in 2002. His love of basketball inspired the story for the movie he starred in, Like Mike.

finished a script for Fox, and everyone wanted Shad to star in it. "He loves basketball, loves Michael Jordan and he's an exceptional basketball player. It's every kid's dream to play in the NBA and it's not like 'Big' where he becomes a man. In this case, it's more fun that he stays a kid."

The story of an orphan who discovers a pair of magical sneakers that let him play pro basketball was a good match for Shad. Although the 15-year-old was scarcely over five feet tall, he was a huge fan of the game and felt he had the skills to play against the pros. "I've got a handle like [Allen] Iverson and I shoot like Kobe [Bryant]," he told *Sports Illustrated.*

Like Mike was set to premiere on the Fourth of July weekend in 2002, competing against *Men in Black II,* a movie starring another hip-hop artist turned actor, Will Smith. Despite a much smaller budget, *Like Mike* did well, earning over $13 million its first weekend. It made back its $30 million cost before July was over.

Shad's performance in Like Mike earned him a nomination for a Young Artist Award for Best Leading Young Actor.

Shad had proven himself as an actor as well as a rapper. He was nominated for a Young Artist Award for Best Leading Young Actor. Over the next year, Shad

To promote his albums, Shad makes appearances on shows such as MTV's Total Request Live.

divided his time between the two occupations. He read scripts and met with producers for films while working with top producers like the Neptunes, Bone Crusher, and Lil' Wayne on his third album.

He starred in *Johnson Family Vacation*, playing Cedric the Entertainer's son. The movie was released in

2004. Long before then, Shad decided to drop the *Lil* from his name. He was 16 and almost an adult.

In fact, during the recording process, something happened. It was a normal thing for most boys, but a major problem for a recording star.

Shad's voice changed.

His voice grew deeper — two octaves lower — during the work on his third album. Although the incident stretched the time it took to finish the album, Shad didn't think it would hurt his sales. "Some people didn't know it was Bow Wow when they first heard it," he later told Jim Farber of Knight Ridder/Tribune Information Services. "But it didn't change my flow and that's what matters."

As a teenager, Shad understands how difficult the transition is going to be. Very few child stars continue in the field as adults. As a movie actor Shad could look to Jodie Foster or Drew Barrymore, who started as a toddlers and have been top actresses for decades. Many think Shad is growing up like Michael Jackson did.

As a teenager, Shad understands how difficult the transition will be from kid rapper to adult artist.

Whether or not Shad can manage the record sales of Jackson, without the drama, remains to be seen. In Au-

Shad not only makes albums and movies, he also has a clothing line. Here he wears a jersey from his Shago clothing line.

gust 2003, his third CD, *Unleashed,* was released. In its first two months in stores, it sold over 500,000 copies. He also launched his own clothing line, called Shago, in June 2003. Changing his name and changing his voice hasn't seemed to change his fans' minds.

CHRONOLOGY

1987	born Shad Gregory Moss on March 9 in Columbus, Ohio
1993	joins Snoop Dogg's The Chronic Tour; appears on Snoop's album *Doggystyle*
1994-98	returns to Columbus, Ohio; attends Reynoldsburg Elementary and Junior High Schools
1998	signs with Sony Records' Epic label; begins working with producer Jermaine Dupri
2000	debut CD *Beware of Dog* sells over two million copies; headlines Scream Tour
2001	follow-up CD, *Doggy Bag,* sells over one million copies
2002	stars in movie *Like Mike;* drops *Lil* from *Bow Wow*
2003	releases third album, *Unleashed*
2004	stars in *Johnson Family Vacation*

FOR FURTHER READING

Books:

Cassata, Mary Anne. *Lil Bow Wow Scrapbook.* New York: Random House, 2001.

Johns, Michale-Anne. *Hangin' With Lil Bow Wow.* New York: Scholastic, 2002.

On the Web:

Bow Wow (Official Site)
http://www.lilbowwow.com/

Launch – Bow Wow: Artist Page
http://www.launch.yahoo.com/artist/
default.asp?artistID=1048320

MTV Bands A-Z: Bow Wow
http://www.mtv.com/bands/az/bow_wow/artist.jhtml

Albums
2000   *Beware of Dog*
2001   *Doggy Bag*
2003   *Unleashed*

Selected Singles
2000   "Bounce With Me"
2001   "Bow Wow (That's My Name)"
2001   "Take Ya Home"
2001   "Puppy Love"
2001   "Ghetto Girls"
2003   "Let's Get Down"
2003   "My Baby"

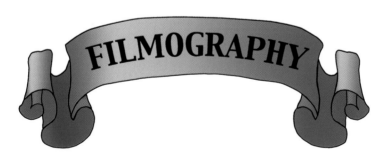

2001   *Carmen: A Hip Hopera* (TV)
2002   *Party in the Park*
2002   *All About the Benjamins*
2002   *Like Mike*
2004   *Johnson Family Vacation*

INDEX